# When You Were Baptized

Catherine Maresca

Illustrated by
Nathan Röhlander

**LTP**
LITURGY
TRAINING
PUBLICATIONS

# This book is presented to

_____,

## baptized on

_____.

_Nihil Obstat_
Rev. Mr. Daniel G. Welter, JD
Chancellor
Archdiocese of Chicago
April 8, 2019

_Imprimatur_
Most Reverend Ronald A. Hicks
Vicar General
Archdiocese of Chicago
April 8, 2019

The _Nihil Obstat_ and _Imprimatur_ are declarations that the material is free from doctrinal or moral error, and thus is granted permission to publish in accordance with c. 827. No legal responsibility is assumed by the grant of this permission. No implication is contained herein that those who have granted the _Nihil Obstat_ and _Imprimatur_ agree with the content, opinions, or statements expressed.

Illustration on p. 9 based on illumination of the Baptism of Christ in the _Life of Christ_, courtesy of the British Library, Harley 4328.

Stained glass window image references from The Crosiers/Gene Plaisted, osc.

Interior and exterior church architecture was inspired by Holy Family Church, South Pasadena, CA. Illustration on p. 16 was inspired by a photograph taken by Maria Laughlin, St. James Cathedral, Seattle, WA.

This book was edited by Michaela I. Tudela. Víctor R. Pérez was the production editor. Design and art direction by Anna Manhart.

Art © Nathan Röhlander

23 22 21 20 19    1 2 3 4 5

Printed in the United States of America.

Library of Congress Control Number: 2019934259

ISBN 978-1-61671-496-3

EWB

With gratitude to Sofia Cavalletti and the many children
who have taught me to treasure the signs of Baptism.

~C.M.


With love to Amy, and for our boys Sixten and Soren.
May they grow in spirit and strength.

~N.R.

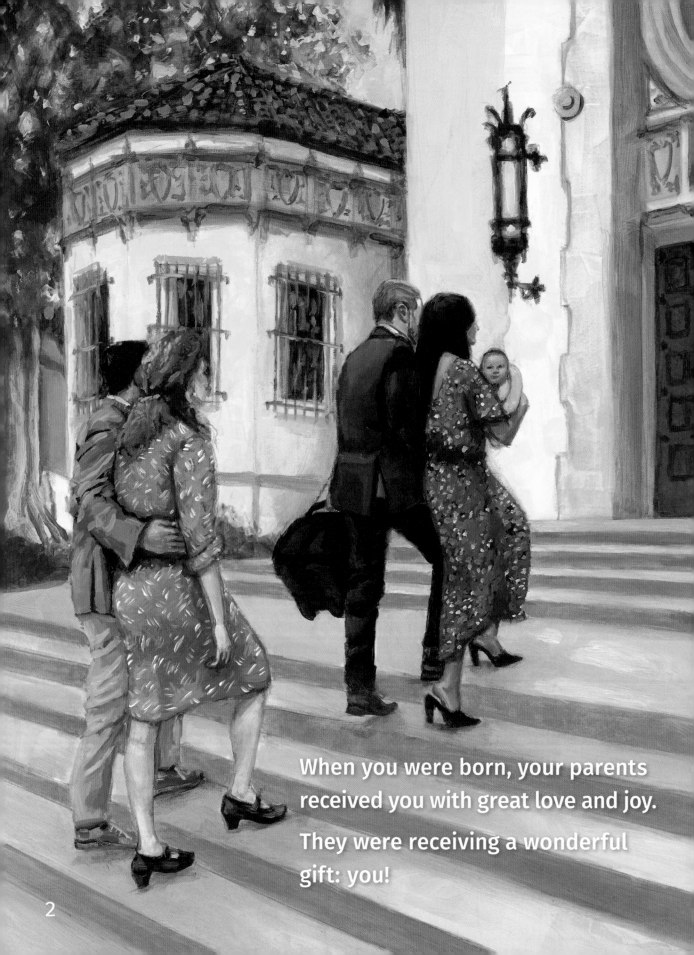

When you were born, your parents received you with great love and joy.

They were receiving a wonderful gift: you!

2

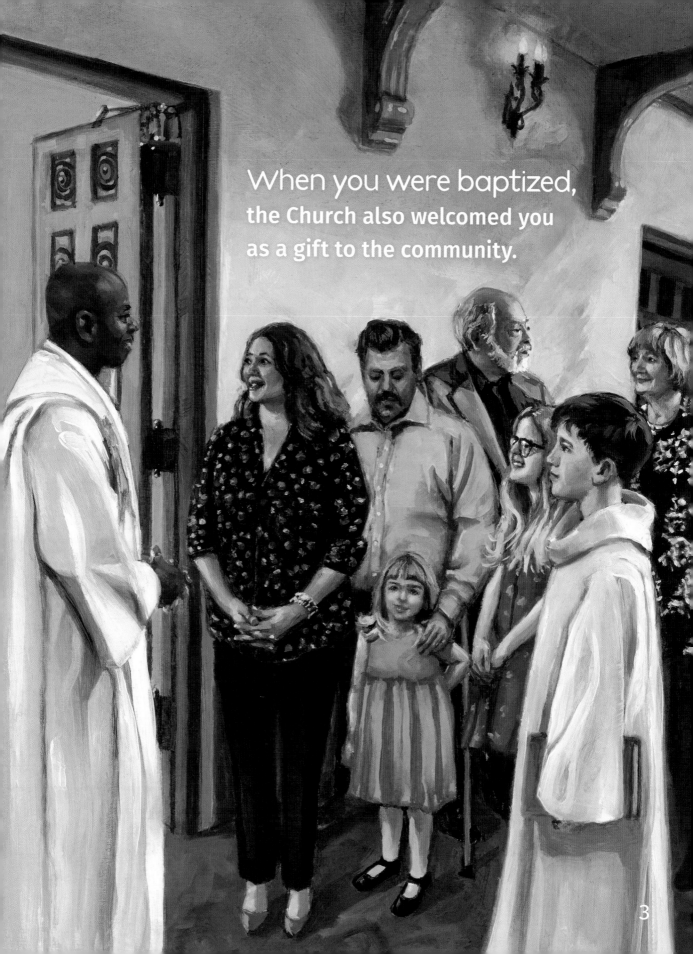

When you were baptized,
the Church also welcomed you
as a gift to the community.

3

Jesus, our Good
Shepherd, calls you
by your name.

Your name tells us
who you are and who
your family is.

4

When you were baptized, your parents announced the name they chose for you.

The priest called you by your name to welcome you, to baptize you with the water, and to give you Christ's light.

5

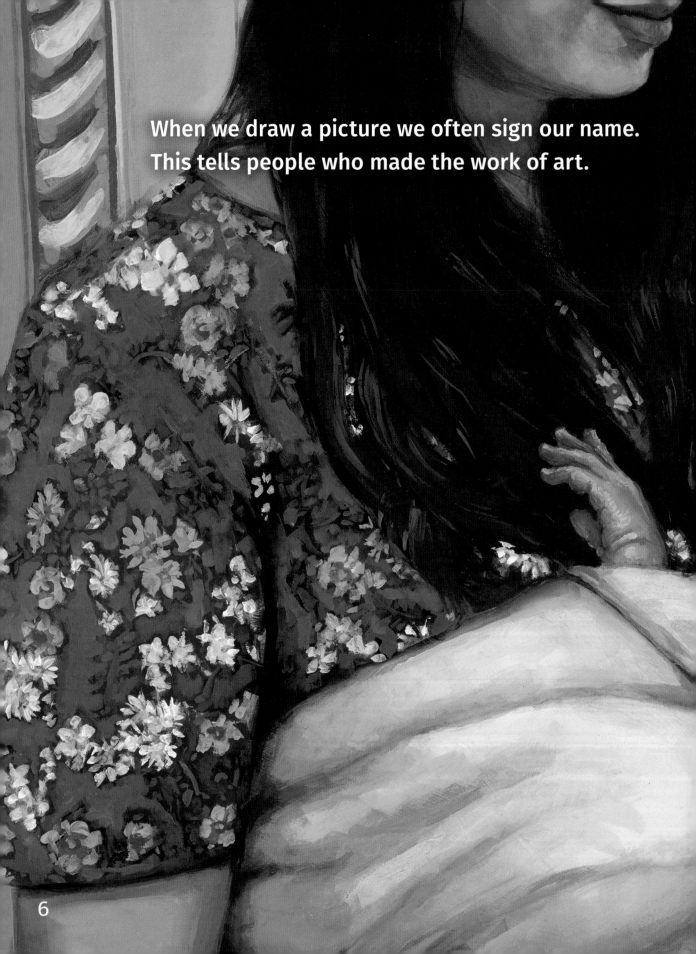

When we draw a picture we often sign our name.
This tells people who made the work of art.

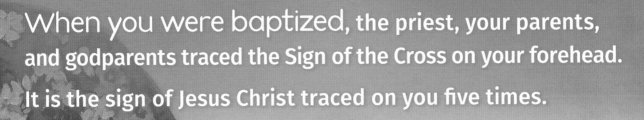

When you were baptized, the priest, your parents, and godparents traced the Sign of the Cross on your forehead.

It is the sign of Jesus Christ traced on you five times.

YOU are God's work of art!

Our parents say words of love to us. We hear words of help and healing from those who care for us. When we hear these loving words, we feel strong.

When you were baptized, everyone listened to the Word of God. Through the Holy Bible, God also gives you words of love, of help, and of healing to help you live in God's joy.

When you were baptized, those gathered at your church that day prayed for you and your parents.

Even the saints in heaven prayed for you to grow in faith.

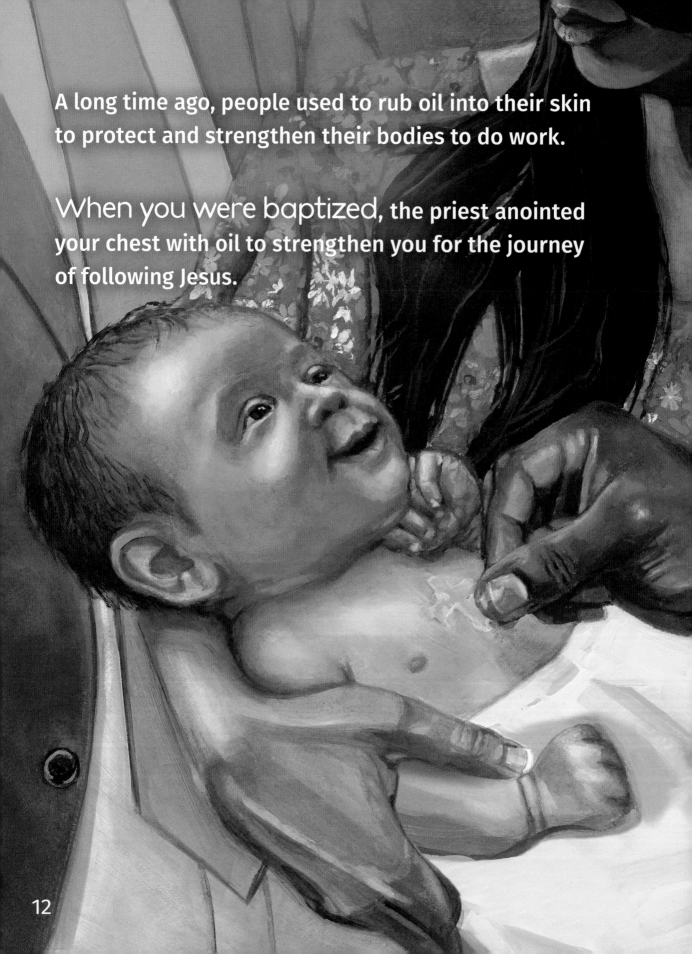

A long time ago, people used to rub oil into their skin to protect and strengthen their bodies to do work.

When you were baptized, the priest anointed your chest with oil to strengthen you for the journey of following Jesus.

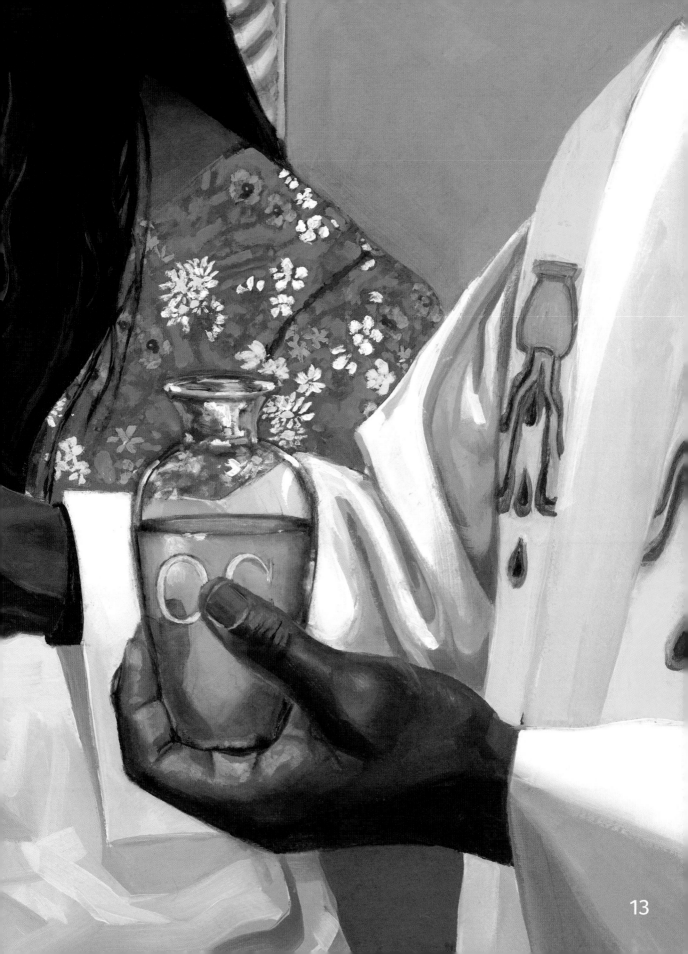

We use our
hands to call
each other
to us to share
a hug and
celebrate
our love.

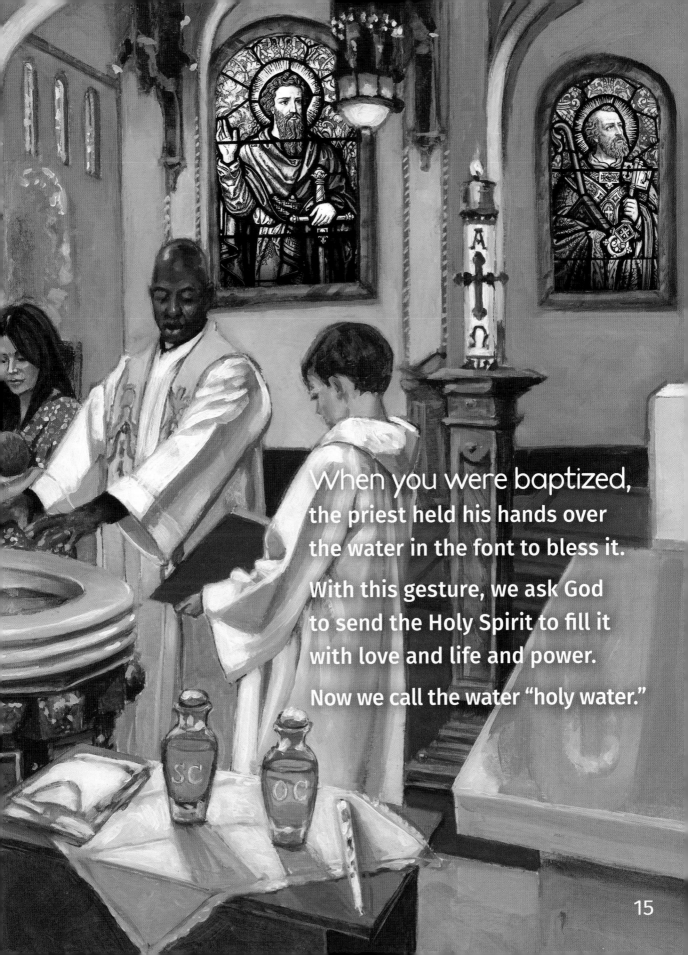

When you were baptized, the priest held his hands over the water in the font to bless it.

With this gesture, we ask God to send the Holy Spirit to fill it with love and life and power.

Now we call the water "holy water."

15

How do we use water every day? We water our plants. We fill the water bowls of our pets. They need water to live. We drink water to live, too. We also use water to wash and clean ourselves.

**"I baptize you in the name of the Father, and of the Son, and of the Holy Spirit."**

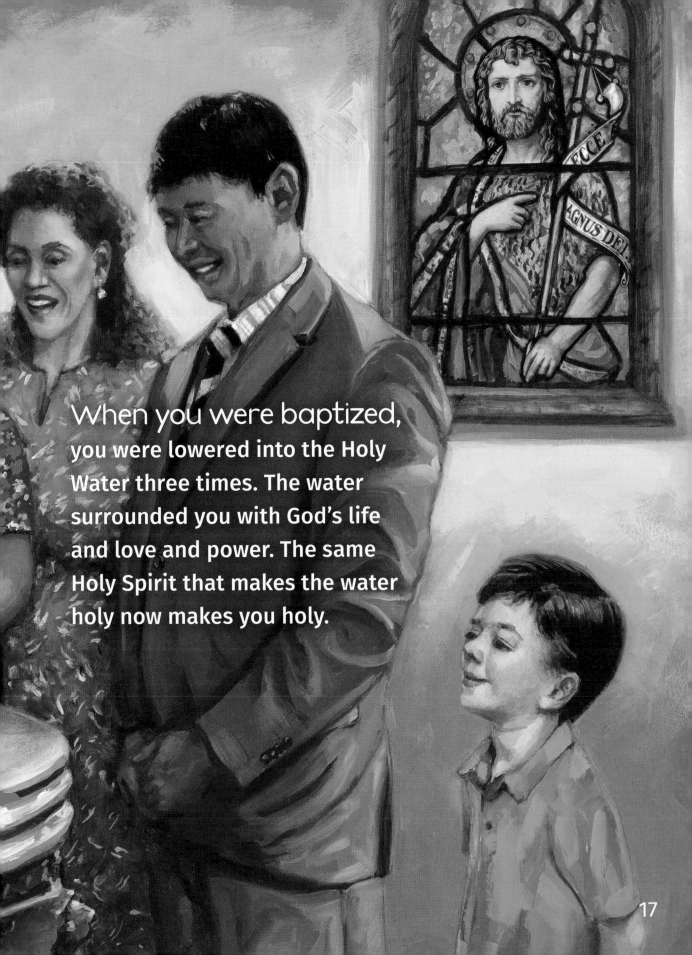

When you were baptized, you were lowered into the Holy Water three times. The water surrounded you with God's life and love and power. The same Holy Spirit that makes the water holy now makes you holy.

The lovely scent of this perfumed oil spreads in the air, bringing joy to others.

When you were baptized, your head was anointed with this sweet-smelling oil as a sign of our joy. This joy is shared with the Church and the world just like perfume. It reminds us of the joy that Jesus brings to us every day.

Some clothes show that we belong to a school or a team. Sometimes what we wear tells others who we are.

When you were baptized, the Church gave you a white garment to welcome you to the altar, and to remind you that you belong to Jesus and are full of his light.

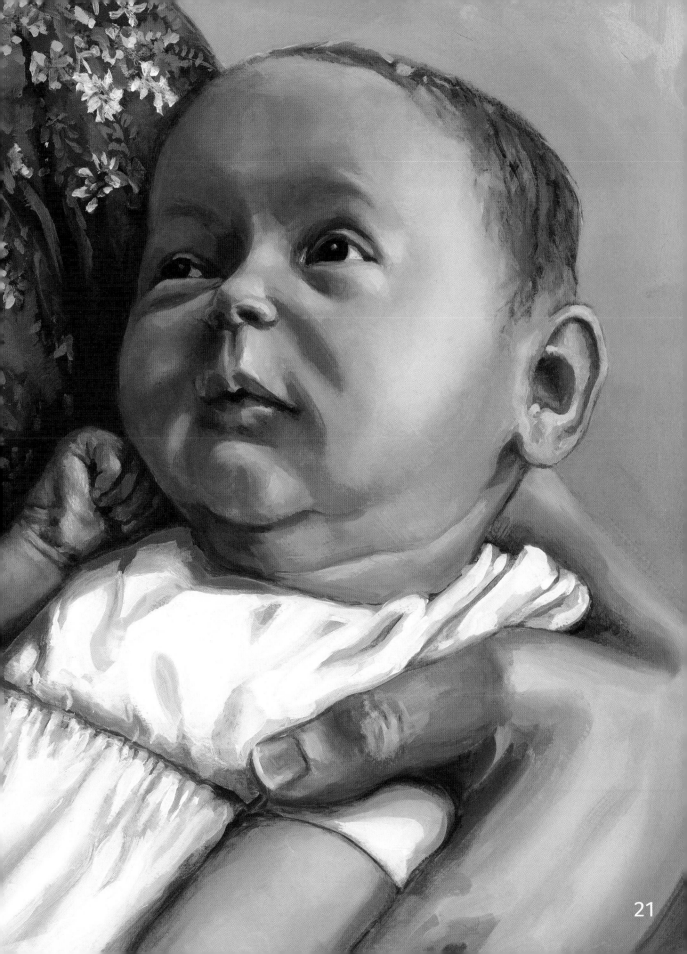

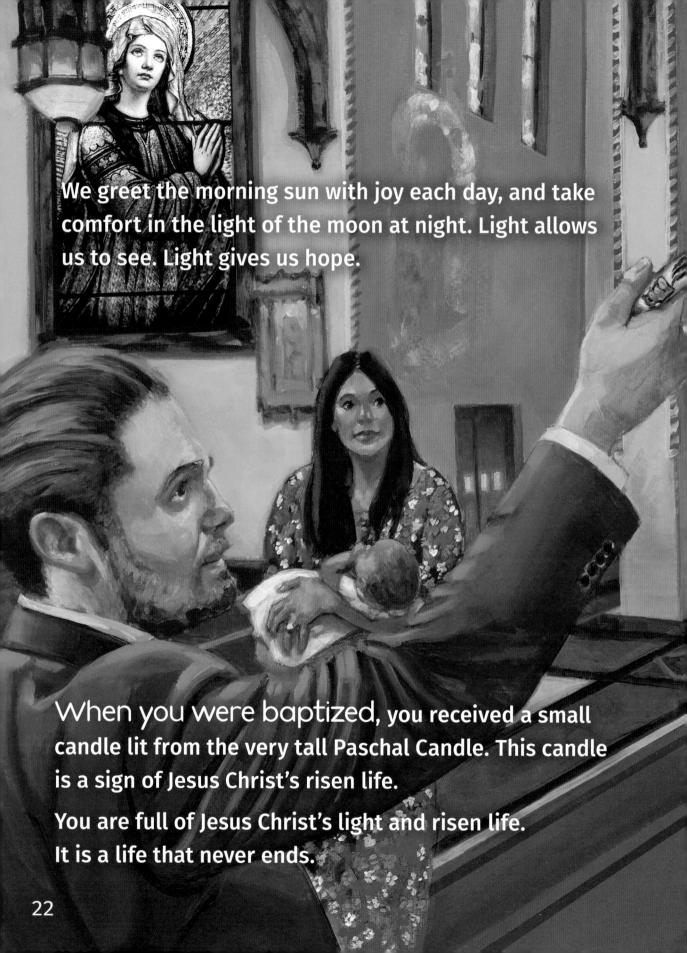

We greet the morning sun with joy each day, and take comfort in the light of the moon at night. Light allows us to see. Light gives us hope.

When you were baptized, you received a small candle lit from the very tall Paschal Candle. This candle is a sign of Jesus Christ's risen life.

You are full of Jesus Christ's light and risen life.
It is a life that never ends.

Do you have a favorite song you like to sing?
What story do you like to listen to every night?

Every family has some special prayers and
stories you hear again and again.

You are learning your family's own stories.

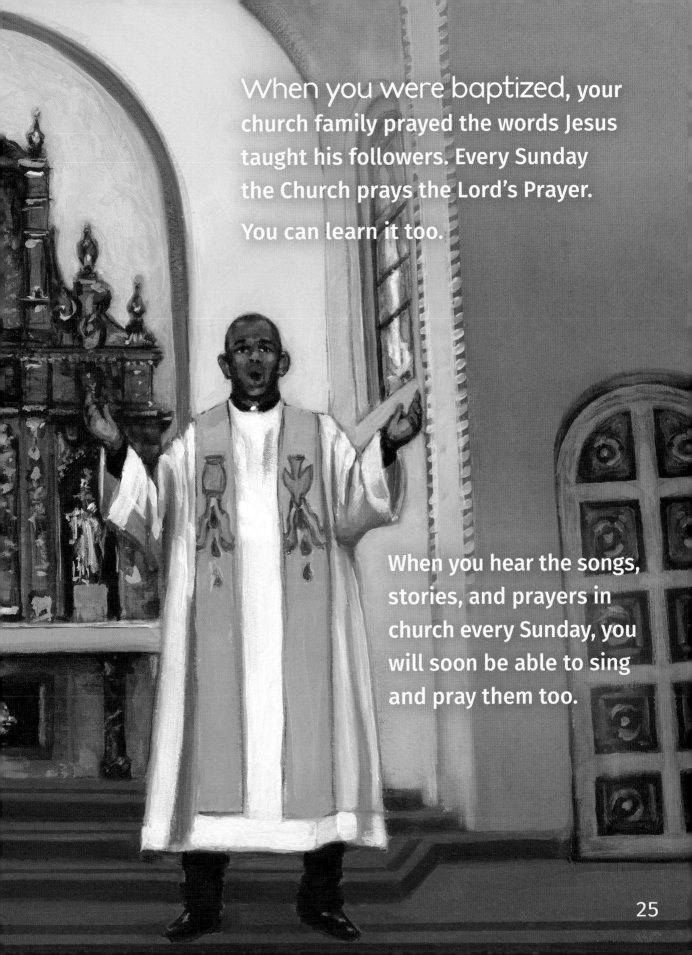

When you were baptized, your church family prayed the words Jesus taught his followers. Every Sunday the Church prays the Lord's Prayer.

You can learn it too.

When you hear the songs, stories, and prayers in church every Sunday, you will soon be able to sing and pray them too.

When you were baptized, your parents and friends received a gift, a blessing. The priest prayed for your parents, thanking God for you and asking God to help your parents as they help you to grow.

Then the priest asked God to bless all your friends at church when you were baptized.

This community helps you grow as one of God's children, full of God's light and life.

Have your parents ever blessed you, asking God
to protect you and keep you safe?

You received so many gifts when you were baptized:
your name, the Bible, oil, water, Christ's light, and more.

These will be yours for the rest of your life.

# Note for Parents

The gifts of the Church at Baptism are rooted in the natural and human gifts of God and family. They grow in meaning as biblical signs, and finally take on the meaning of their life in the Church. For example, light is necessary for life and enables us to see. In the Bible, light is the first gift of creation, is used to guide the Israelites into freedom, and is an image of Jesus Christ, the Messiah. In the church, we light the Paschal and baptismal candles as a sign of risen life. We light the sanctuary lamp as a sign of God's presence with us in the tabernacle. We also often hold candles near the Gospel as a sign of God's teaching to us in the Word.

While the Baptism depicted in this book shows the child being immersed in holy water, Baptism may take place either by immersion or by pouring water on the head. Immersion, however, is a more vivid way to show cleansing from sin and rebirth in Christ. Afterward, the anointing with chrism on the crown of the head takes place. This anointing means more than spreading joy, though we are called by our Baptism to spread the Gospel message and to bring hope to others. With older children and adults, we introduce that in the Old Testament, priests, prophets, and kings were anointed with oil to signify the presence of God's Spirit within them. Your child was consecrated to take on the same important responsibilities of priest, prophet, and king. This way of looking at discipleship can be taught to very young children by talking about sacrifice and sharing (priesthood), telling the truth (prophet), and taking care of everyone before yourself (kingship).

For children younger than six, whose biblical knowledge and liturgical experience are still growing, the gifts of Baptism presented here are rooted in natural and human life, and together point to the abundant generosity of God as your child is welcomed into the Church. Note that we respect the spirituality of the young child, characterized by joy, wonder, and love. They are not concerned, or even able to be concerned, with moral considerations until after age six. Baptism is a sacrament that welcomes us and prepares us for life in God. Each gift received on the day of Baptism will grow in meaning and purpose as your child grows. Your child was not baptized in fear, but in faith, anticipating the powerful work of God in his or her life.

**Catherine Maresca** is founder and director of the Center for Children and Theology in Washington, DC, where she researches the spiritual life of children and prepares resources for children and adults. She has been a catechist in the Catechesis of the Good Shepherd for thirty-two years at Christian Family Montessori School and has been training catechists since 1985. Among the many books and articles she has written and edited on the spirituality of children, Catherine is also the author of *Violence and Nonviolence in Scripture: Helping Children Understand Challenging Stories* (Liturgy Training Publications).

**Nathan Röhlander** is a fine artist, illustrator, and adjunct professor at the Art Center College of Design in Pasadena, California, where he teaches Composition and Drawing, and Composition and Painting. Nathan is married to Amy and they are the proud parents of two boys, Sixten Oak and Soren Hawk. All three are depicted in this book.